Animals in Danger!

Polar Bears

Nancy Dickmann

Brown Bear Books

Published by Brown Bear Books Ltd
4877 N. Circulo Bujia
Tucson, AZ 85718
USA

and

Unit 1/D, Leroy House
436 Essex Rd
London N1 3QP
UK

© 2019 Brown Bear Books Ltd

ISBN 978-1-78121-443-5 (library bound)
ISBN 978-1-78121-465-7 (paperback)

All rights reserved. No part of this book may be reproduced, stored in a retrieval system or transmitted in any form or by any means, electronic, mechanical, photocopying, recording or otherwise, without the prior written permission of the copyright holder.

Library of Congress Cataloging-in-Publication Data available on request

Text: Nancy Dickmann
Designer: Supriya Sahai
Design Manager: Keith Davis
Picture Researcher: Laila Torsun
Editorial Director: Lindsey Lowe
Children's Publisher: Anne O'Daly

Manufactured in the United States of America
CPSIA compliance information: Batch#AG/5623

Picture Credits
The photographs in this book are used by permission and through the courtesy of:

Front Cover: Shutterstock: Vaclav Sebek.
123rf: Iakov Filimonov 1; Dreamstime: Andreanita 12, Ggw1962 16, Lori H 18; Getty Images: Paul Nicklen, 16–17; iStock: andylewisphoto 14, atese 10, Kristian Septimus Krogh, 21, John Pitcher 5, 10–11; Shutterstock: Heather M. Davidson 8, Florida Stock 14–15, 18–19, 20, Ilyas Kamilmullin 4, Alexey Seafarer 12–13, Vaclav Sebek 9, Elena Shchipkova 6–7.

All other artwork and photography
© Brown Bear Books.

t-top, r-right, l-left, c-center, b-bottom

Brown Bear Books has made every attempt to contact the copyright holder. If you have any information please contact:
licensing@brownbearbooks.co.uk

Websites
The website addresses in this book were valid at the time of going to press. However, it is possible that contents or addresses may change following publication of this book. No responsibility for any such changes can be accepted by the author or the publisher. Readers should be supervised when they access the Internet.

Words in **bold** appear in the Useful Words on page 23.

Contents

What Are Polar Bears?................ 4
Polar Bear Habitats 6
Surviving in Snow 8
Ice Hunters 10
Polar Bear Cubs 12
Polar Bears in Danger 14
Helping Polar Bears 16
What's Next? 18
Polar Bear Helpers 20
Fact File 21
Try It! 22
Useful Words 23
Find Out More 24
Index 24

What Are Polar Bears?

Polar bears are large **mammals**. They are related to grizzly bears and pandas. Their bodies are covered in fur. They make milk for their babies. Polar bears walk on four legs. They are also good swimmers.

Polar bears are the largest type of bear.

IN DANGER!
Polar bears are in danger of dying out. People need to protect them.

Polar bears are **predators**. They hunt other animals to eat. But no animals hunt polar bears.

Polar Bear Habitats

A **habitat** is a place where an animal lives. Polar bears live in the **Arctic**. There is a large ocean there. Much of the ocean is covered in ice.

Arctic Ocean

The Arctic is the area around the North Pole. It is cold all year round.

WOW! Temperatures in the **Arctic** can be below –58°F (–50°C).

The Arctic warms up a little in the summer.
Some of the ice melts. It breaks into pieces.
Polar bears live partly on land and partly on ice.

Surviving in Snow

Polar bears can survive on snow and ice. They have strong, sharp claws. These can grip and dig through ice. Rough skin keeps polar bear feet from slipping.

Furry paws protect feet from the cold ground.

WOW!

A polar bear's white color blends in with the snow.

A thick coat of fur keeps a polar bear warm. There is a layer of fat under the skin. It helps keep body heat in.

Ice Hunters

Polar bears mostly eat seals. They hunt them on the sea ice. When the ice melts, polar bears can't hunt.

WOW! Polar bears can smell a seal from 0.6 miles (1 km) away!

Polar bears often hunt ringed seals.

Seals need to breathe air. They come to holes in the ice. A polar bear waits near a hole. When a seal appears, the bear grabs it.

Polar Bear Cubs

Baby polar bears are called cubs. A mother polar bear digs a den in the snow. Her cubs are born there. They drink milk from their mother. The milk is very rich.

A den keeps the cubs warm and safe.

After a few months, the cubs leave the den.
They follow their mother to the sea ice.
The cubs learn how to hunt by watching her.

Polar Bears in Danger

Polar bears are at risk of dying out.
They need sea ice to hunt and raise cubs.
But Earth's **climate** is getting warmer.
This means there is less sea ice.
It melts earlier in the year.

Burning some **fuels** releases a gas into the air. This traps the Sun's heat.

Without sea ice, polar bears cannot hunt. They might starve. We must keep Earth from getting any warmer. Using less electricity will help. So will driving less.

Helping Polar Bears

Scientists want to learn about polar bears. If there is little sea ice, polar bears may come on land. They may come into towns, looking for food.

Polar bears are big and strong. They can be very dangerous.

Scientists put radio collars on polar bears.
The collars send a signal. It shows where a bear is.
Scientists can see were the bears go to find food.

What's Next?

There are about 26,000 polar bears left. Their numbers are going down. People have made laws to help polar bears. There are laws to protect their **habitat**, too.

There is oil beneath the Arctic Ocean. Drilling for it could harm polar bears.

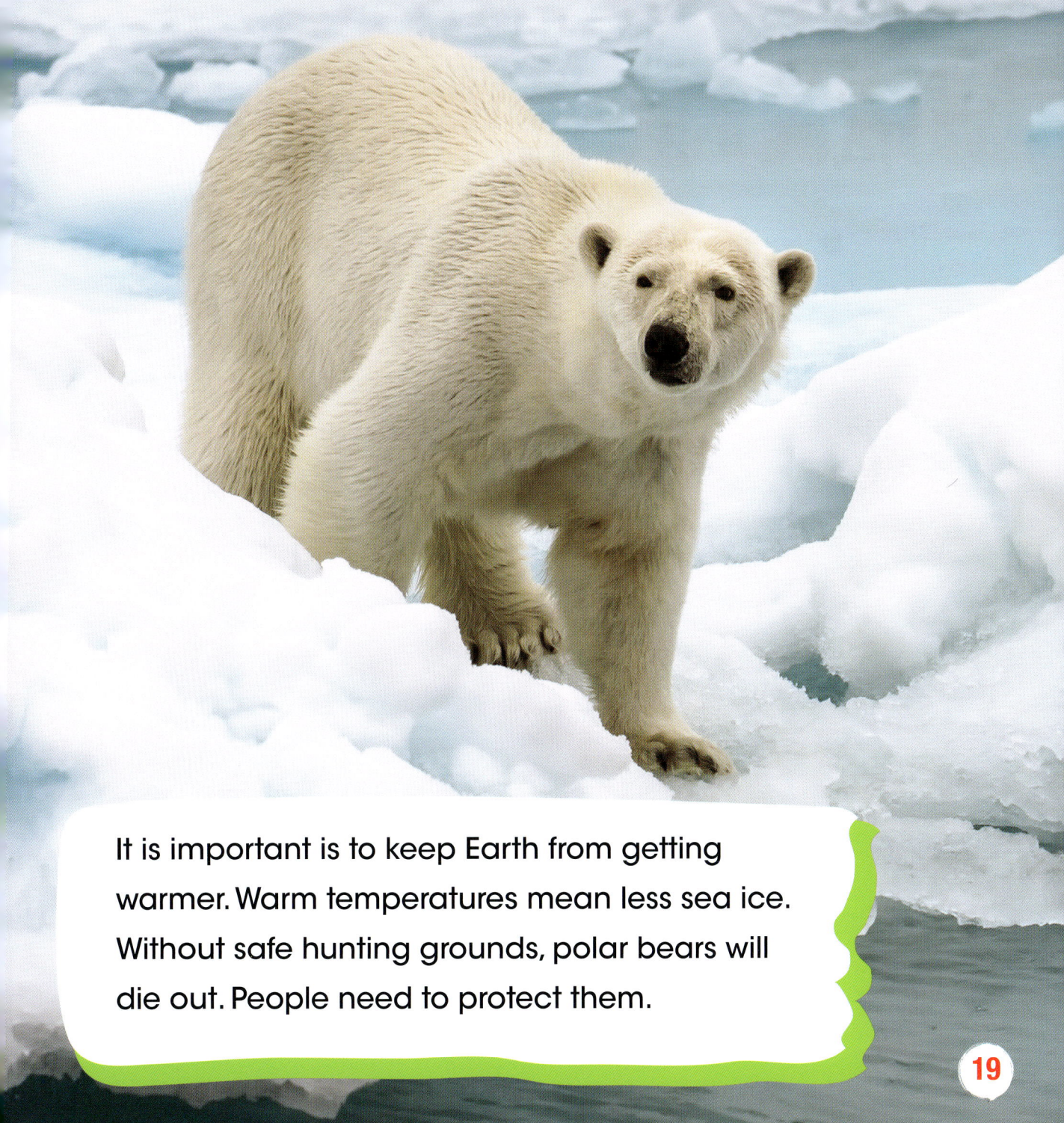

It is important is to keep Earth from getting warmer. Warm temperatures mean less sea ice. Without safe hunting grounds, polar bears will die out. People need to protect them.

Polar Bear Helpers

These groups help polar bears:

The International Union for Conservation of Nature (IUCN) is a group of scientists. The scientists count animals. They keep track of their numbers. They decide whether an animal is **endangered**. They say when it has gone **extinct**.

Polar Bears International is a charity. It works to protect the **Arctic**.

The WWF is a charity. It helps protect polar bears' **habitat**.

Fact File

Average life span: 25–30 years

Size: up to 8 feet (2.4 meters) long

Weight: up to 1,600 pounds (725 kilograms)

Diet: mainly seals

Running speed: 30 miles (48 kilometers) per hour

WOW! One polar bear swam for nine days. She covered 400 miles (644 kilometers)!

Try It!

Imagine that you are a scientist. You are tracking a mother bear and her cubs. What do they eat? Make a pictograph to show the results.

You will need:
- graph paper
- pencil
- ruler
- colored pencils

1. Make a table with two columns. The second column should be wider.

2. Write "Food" above the first column. Write "Number eaten" above the second.

3. Choose a symbol for each food type. You could use a drawing of the animal.

4. For each line, draw symbols to show the number eaten. One symbol equals one animal. Which row is longest?

Food Type	Number
Bearded seals	2
Reindeer	1
Ringed seals	9
Seabirds	4
Walruses	1

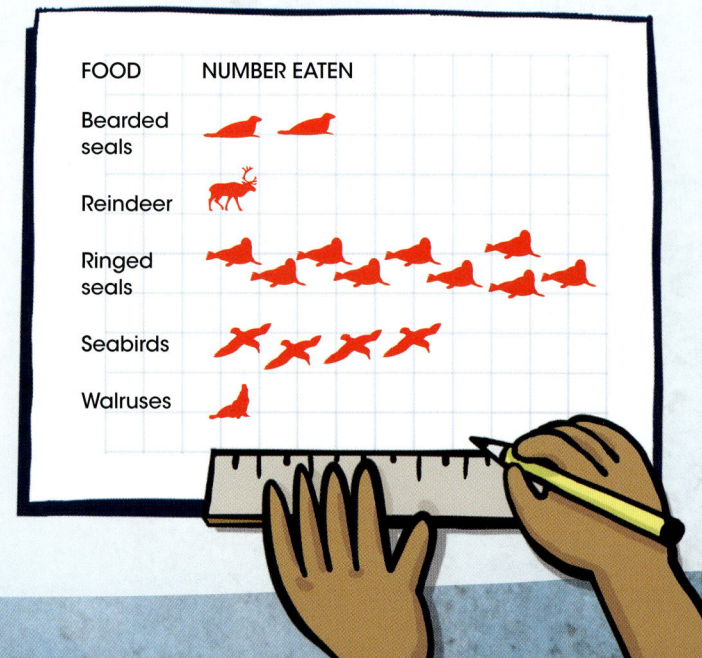

Useful Words

Arctic The land and sea surrounding the North Pole. It is very cold.

climate The average weather in a place over a long period of time.

endangered In danger of dying out completely so that no more will be left.

extinct Having died out completely so that no more are left.

fuel Something that can be burned to release energy. Oil, coal, and gas are fuels.

habitat The place where a plant or animal lives.

mammal A group of animals that have fur and make milk for their young.

oil A thick, black, sticky liquid found underground. It can be made into fuel.

predator An animal that hunts other animals to eat.

Find Out More

Websites

www.nationalgeographic.com/animals/mammals/p/polar-bear/

polarbearsinternational.org/polar-bears

www.wwf.org.uk/wildlife/polar-bears

Books

It's a Polar Bear! Kerry Dinmont, Lerner Publishing, 2018

Polar Bears Mark Newman, Square Fish, 2015

Polar Bears Leo Statts, ABDO, 2016

Index

Arctic 6, 7, 18

claws 8
cubs 4, 12, 13, 14

fur 4, 8, 9

habitats 6, 18
hunting 5, 10, 11, 13, 14, 15, 19

ice 6, 7, 8, 10, 11, 14, 15, 16, 19

mammals 4
melting ice 7, 10, 14, 15, 16, 19
milk 4, 12

oil 18

predators 5

radio collars 17

seals 10, 11
snow 8, 12
swimming 4

walrus 10
whales 10